GW01605241

PRABHU-
PASEBAND-

AN ILLUSTRATED GUIDE TO CRICKET

ANJANA PRABHU-PASEBAND

To everyone who enjoys Cricket.

CONTENTS

ACKNOWLEDGMENTS

I GREW UP IN INDIA, WHERE CRICKET IS THE UNOFFICIAL SPORT OF THE NATION. I AM FOREVER THANKFUL TO MY DAD WHO BOUGHT ME MY FIRST CRICKET BAT, A SLAZENGER V 500 WHEN I WAS 9 YEARS OLD. THE BAT SAW A LOT OF BALLS UNTIL IT WAS BROKEN BEYOND USE.

SHREYANSH BOUNCED WITH ENDLESS ENTHUSIASM EVER SINCE THE CONCEPT OF THIS BOOK WAS PUT FORWARD. HE HELPED ME A LOT SHARING HIS IDEAS ON PRESENTING CRICKET.
SAKTHI IS THE WELL-WISHER WHO SUPPORTED MY CRAZY IDEAS WITHOUT WONDERING ABOUT ANY OUTCOMES. THANK YOU, MY FRIEND.
PRAMOD, NITIN, ATUL, DHIRAJ AND AMEY WERE QUITE HELPFUL IN OPTIMISING TECHNICAL CONTENT THAT IS PRESENTED IN THE BOOK.
DEEPNA GAVE ME HOPE ON TODAY'S YOUTH AND CRICKET WHEN SHE EXCELLED IN EXPLAINING FIELDING POSITIONS WITHOUT SLIPPING ANY NAMES. (HA, THE PUN).

THIS BOOK WAS THE RESULT OF PERSISTENT NAGGING OF MY HUSBAND AMEYA. HE LOOKED AFTER MY NOURISHMENT AND ENTERTAINMENT NEEDS DURING THE ONE INTENSE MONTH OF DRAWING CRICKET.

HISTORY OF CRICKET

It is believed that Cricket started off as a game played by shepherd boys in the late 16th century.

The boys used their herding stick and woollen ball to play on sheep-grazed field.

The wicket was often the wicketgate on the fields.

art inspired by “The Young Cricketer” by Francis Cotes, 1768

2019

By 18th century, Cricket was popular among the British upper class and nobility.

Duchesses and Dukes were often seen playing cricket with their friends.

art inspired by "The Cricket Match" by JH Fevit, 1779

Slowly, Cricket marched
to Asia, Africa and America
with the redcoat soldiers of the British empire.

A global governing body of cricket was founded in 1909,
Imperial Cricket Conference which was renamed to
International Cricket Council in 1989.

2019

WHAT IS CRICKET?

Cricket is a bat & ball game played between two teams each having 11 players.

Objective: to score more runs than the other team.

it is played over sections called 'innings' where one team bats and the other bowls.

OBJECTIVE OF THE BATSMAN:
SCORE RUNS BY

HITTING FOUR RUNS

WHEN THE BALL REACHES THE BOUNDARY AFTER TOUCHING THE GROUND

HITTING SIX RUNS

WHEN THE BALL REACHES THE BOUNDARY DIRECTLY OFF THE BAT

OR

RUNNING BETWEEN WICKETS

WHEN THE STRIKER AND NON-STRIKER RUN TOWARDS THE OPPOSITE WICKETS

OBJECTIVE OF THE BOWLER : CHECK 'OUT' SECTION

TO GET THE BATSMAN OUT BY DELIVERING LEGAL DELIVERY OF OVERS*

*OVER : 6 CONSEQUENT DELIVERIES BY THE SAME BOWLER

OBJECTIVE OF THE FIELDER :

TO GET THE BATSMAN OUT BY CONCEDING MINIMUM RUNS

TYPES OF FIELDING

Formats of Cricket

Test Cricket

PLAYED SINCE **1877**

2 INNINGS EACH

5 DAYS

WHITE JERSEY

UNLIMITED OVERS

One Day Internationals

PLAYED SINCE **1971**

1 INNINGS EACH

1 DAY

COLOURFUL JERSEY

50 OVERS

Twenty20

PLAYED SINCE **2005**

1 INNINGS EACH

1 DAY

20 OVERS

Prabhu-Panchamd
2019

PINK BALLS : INTRODUCED IN 2010
FOR BETTER VISIBILITY FOR DAY/NIGHT
TEST MATCHES.

RED BALLS : TRADITIONALLY
USED IN TEST CRICKET.

THE CRICKET GROUND

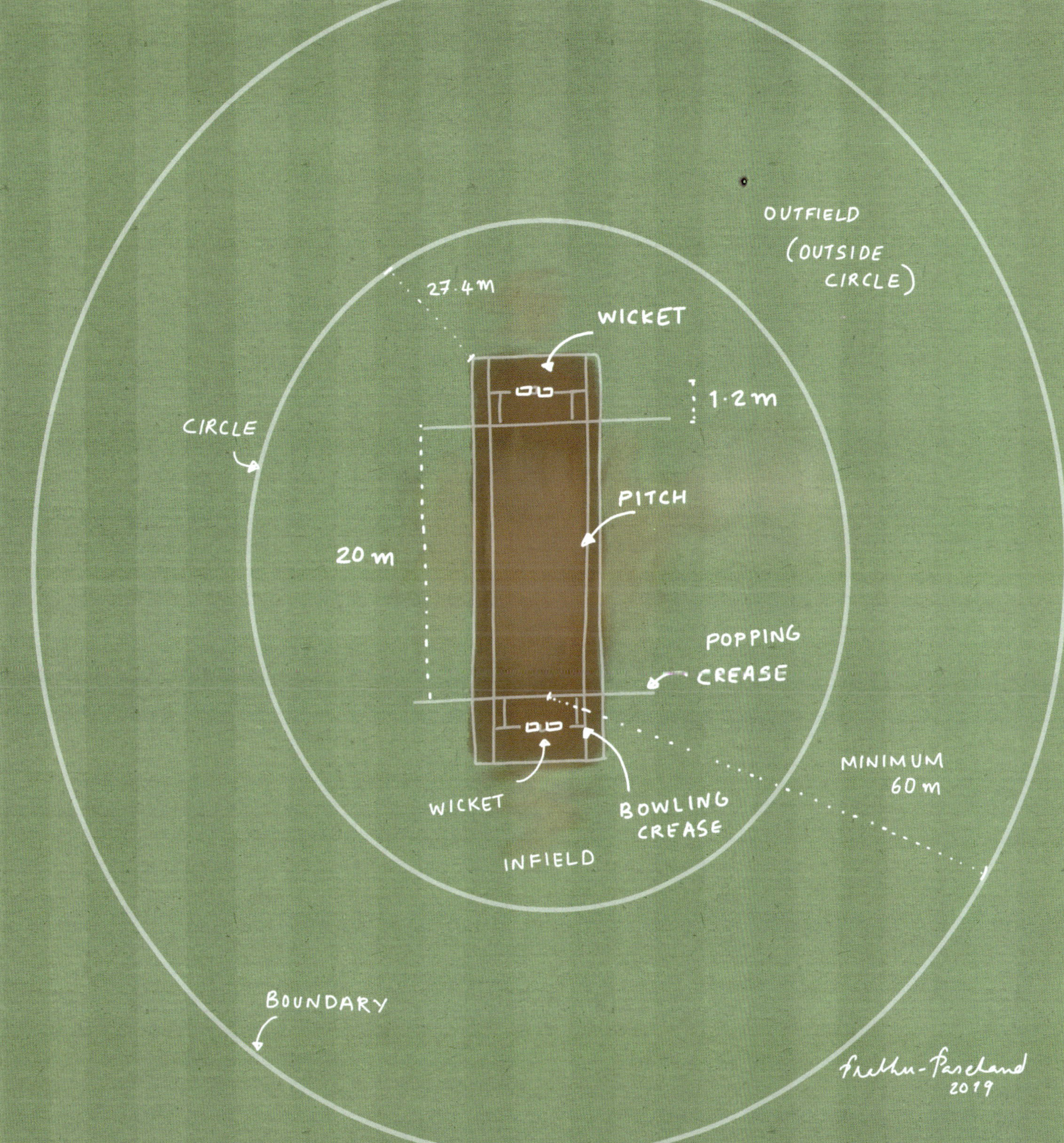
OUTFIELD
(OUTSIDE CIRCLE)
27.4m
WICKET
1.2m
CIRCLE
PITCH
20 m
POPPING
CREASE
MINIMUM
60m
WICKET
BOWLING
CREASE
INFIELD
BOUNDARY
Prabhu-Parekh
2019

FIELDING POSITIONS

POSITIONS OF 9 PLAYERS
ARE DETERMINED ACCORDING
TO BOWLING STRATEGY

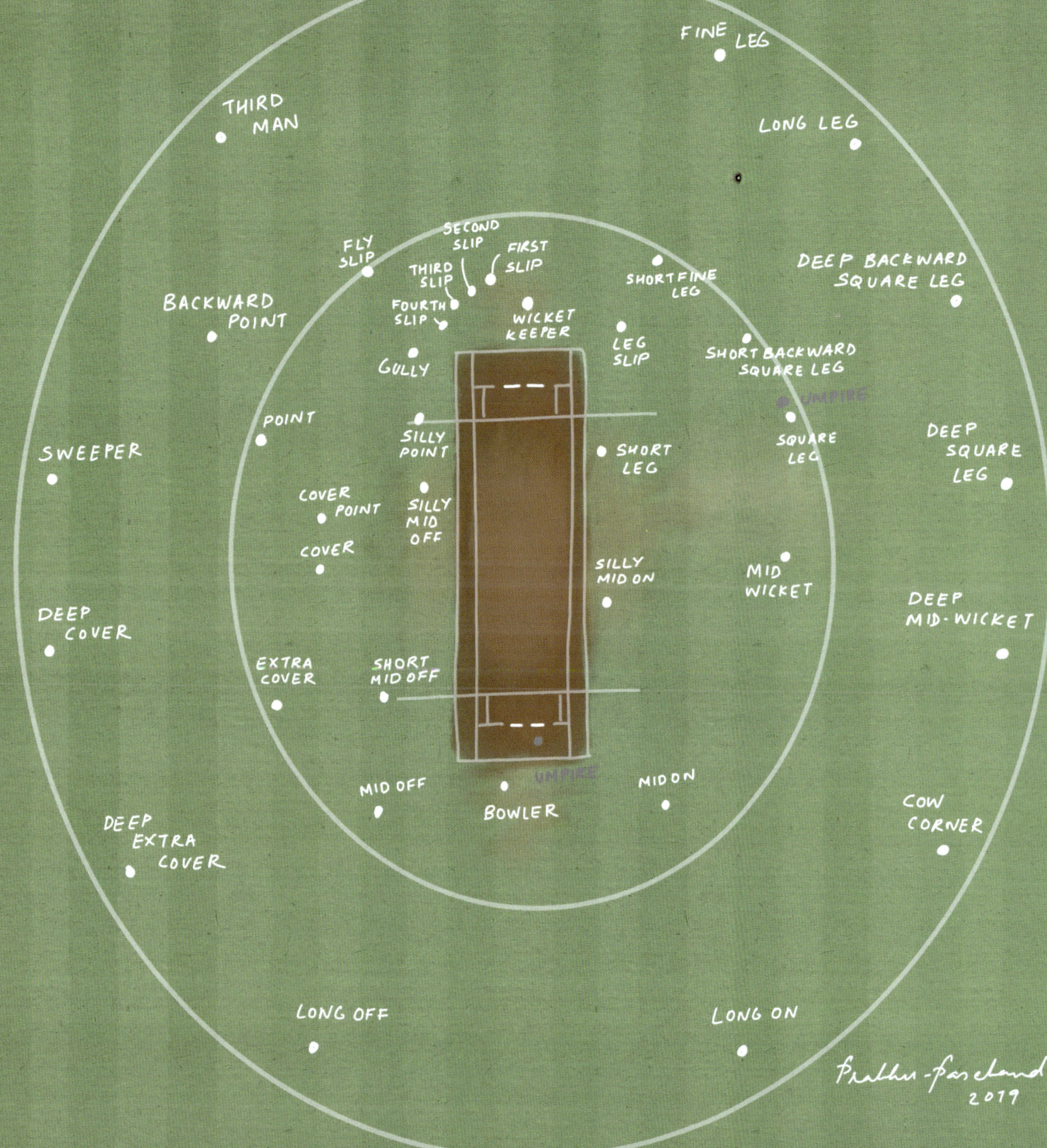
FINE LEG
THIRD MAN
LONG LEG
SECOND SLIP
FLY SLIP
FIRST SLIP
THIRD SLIP
DEEP BACKWARD SQUARE LEG
SHORT FINE LEG
BACKWARD POINT
FOURTH SLIP
WICKET KEEPER
LEG SLIP
SHORT BACKWARD SQUARE LEG
GULLY
UMPIRE
POINT
SILLY POINT
SQUARE LEG
DEEP SQUARE LEG
SWEEPER
SHORT LEG
COVER POINT
SILLY MID OFF
COVER
SILLY MID ON
MID WICKET
DEEP COVER
DEEP MID-WICKET
EXTRA COVER
SHORT MID OFF
UMPIRE
MID OFF
MID ON
BOWLER
COW CORNER
DEEP EXTRA COVER
LONG OFF
LONG ON
2019

BOWLING OVERVIEW

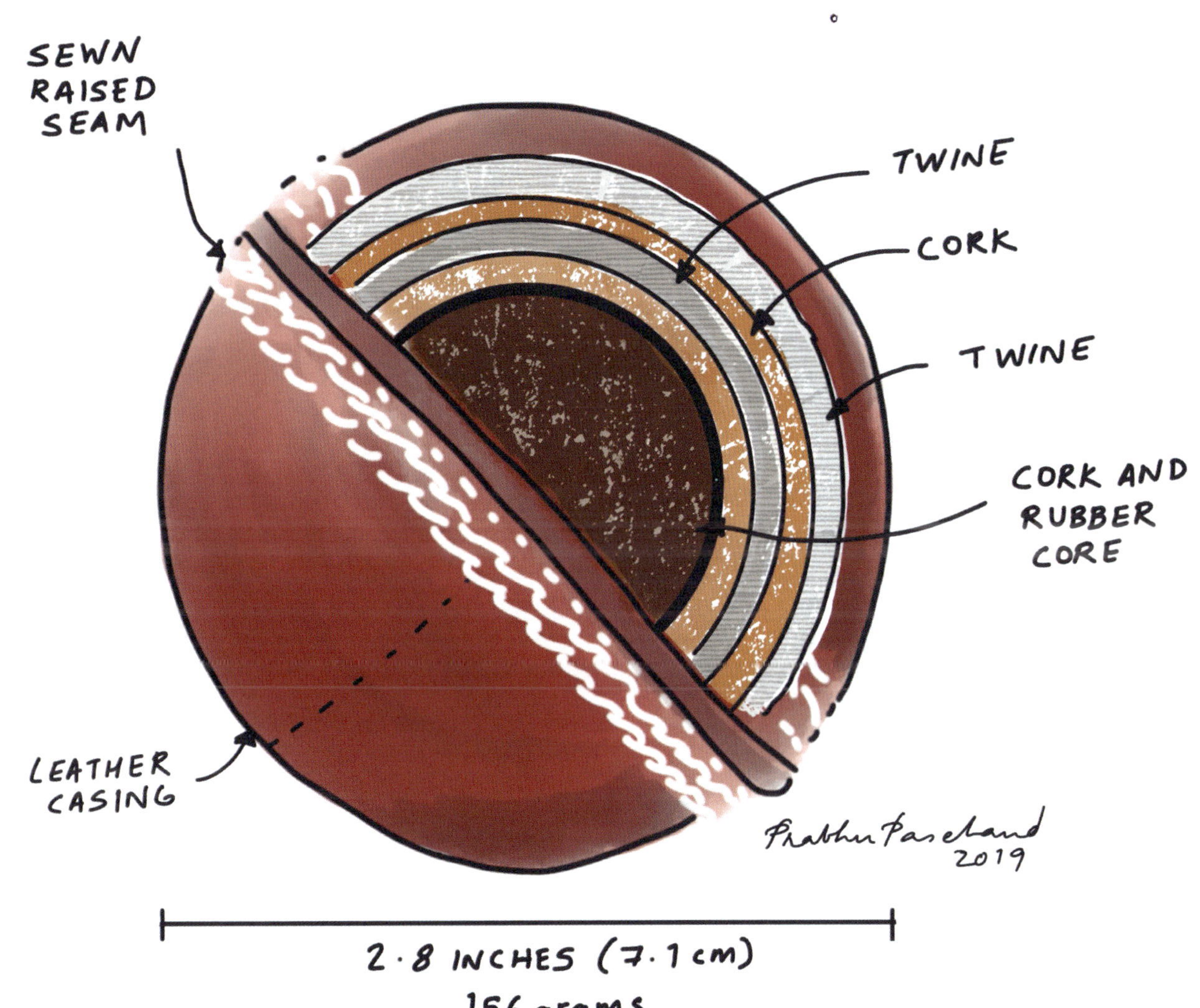
SEWN RAISED SEAM
TWINE
CORK
TWINE
CORK AND RUBBER CORE
LEATHER CASING
2019
2·8 INCHES (7·1 cm)
156 grams

Spin Bowling

Fast Bowling

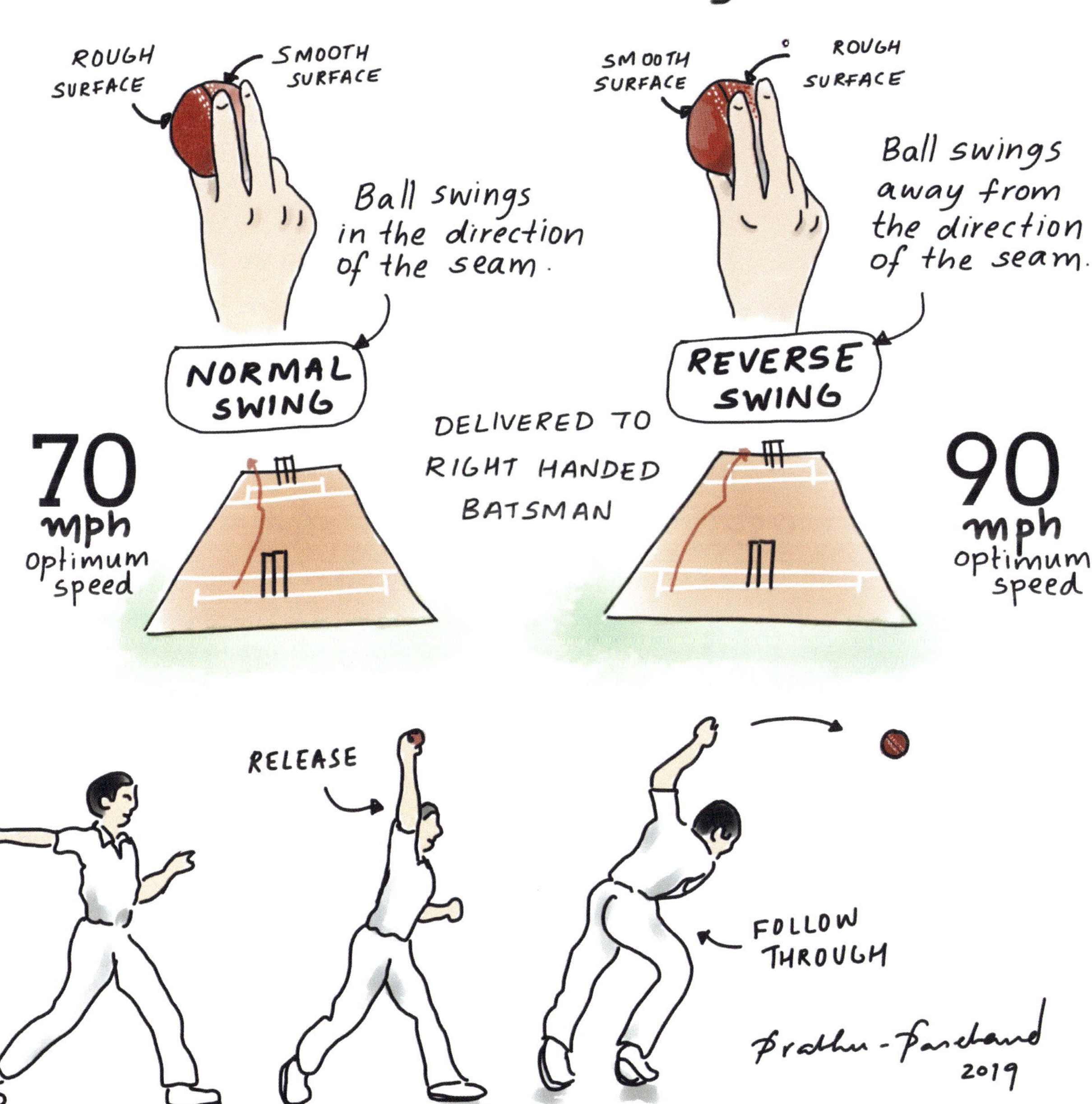

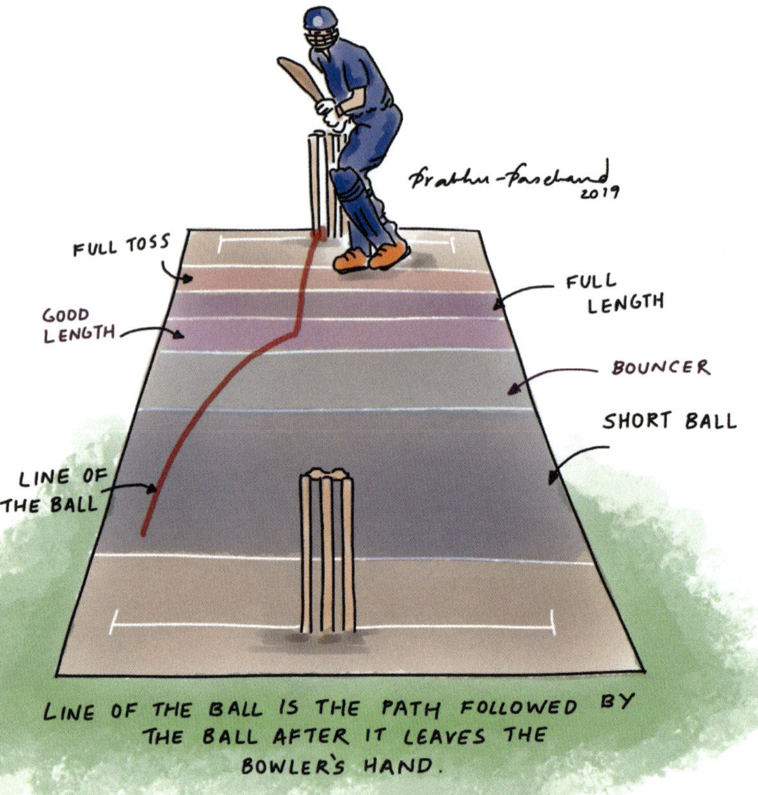
FULL TOSS
GOOD LENGTH
FULL LENGTH
BOUNCER
SHORT BALL
LINE OF THE BALL
LINE OF THE BALL IS THE PATH FOLLOWED BY THE BALL AFTER IT LEAVES THE BOWLER'S HAND.

SLOW BALL
FAST BALL

- THE LONGEST MATCH WAS HELD IN DURBAN IN 1939 BETWEEN SOUTH AFRICA AND ENGLAND WHICH LASTED FOR 12 DAYS.

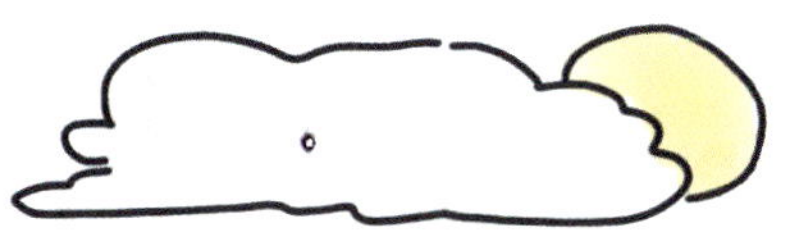

- RAIN AND BAD LIGHT ARE THE MOST COMMON CAUSES FOR DELAYING OR SUSPENDING A MATCH.

- WHEN AUSTRALIA BEAT ENGLAND FOR THE FIRST TIME IN ENGLISH SOIL, AN ENGLISH PAPER SATIRICALLY DUBBED IT AS THE DEATH OF ENGLISH CRICKET AND THE ASHES WERE TAKEN TO AUSTRALIA. THUS BEGAN THE FAMOUS SERIES CALLED 'THE ASHES'.

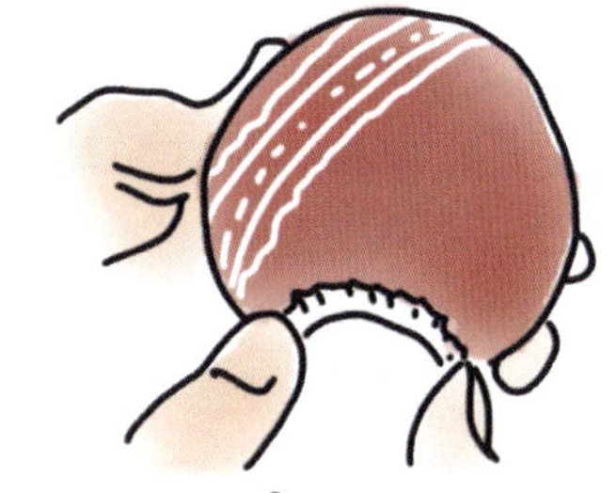

- BALL TAMPERING INCLUDES ILLEGAL ALTERATION OF BALL BY ROUGHENING ONE SIDE TO ALTER THE AERODYNAMIC FEATURES OF THE BALL.

THE EQUIPMENT

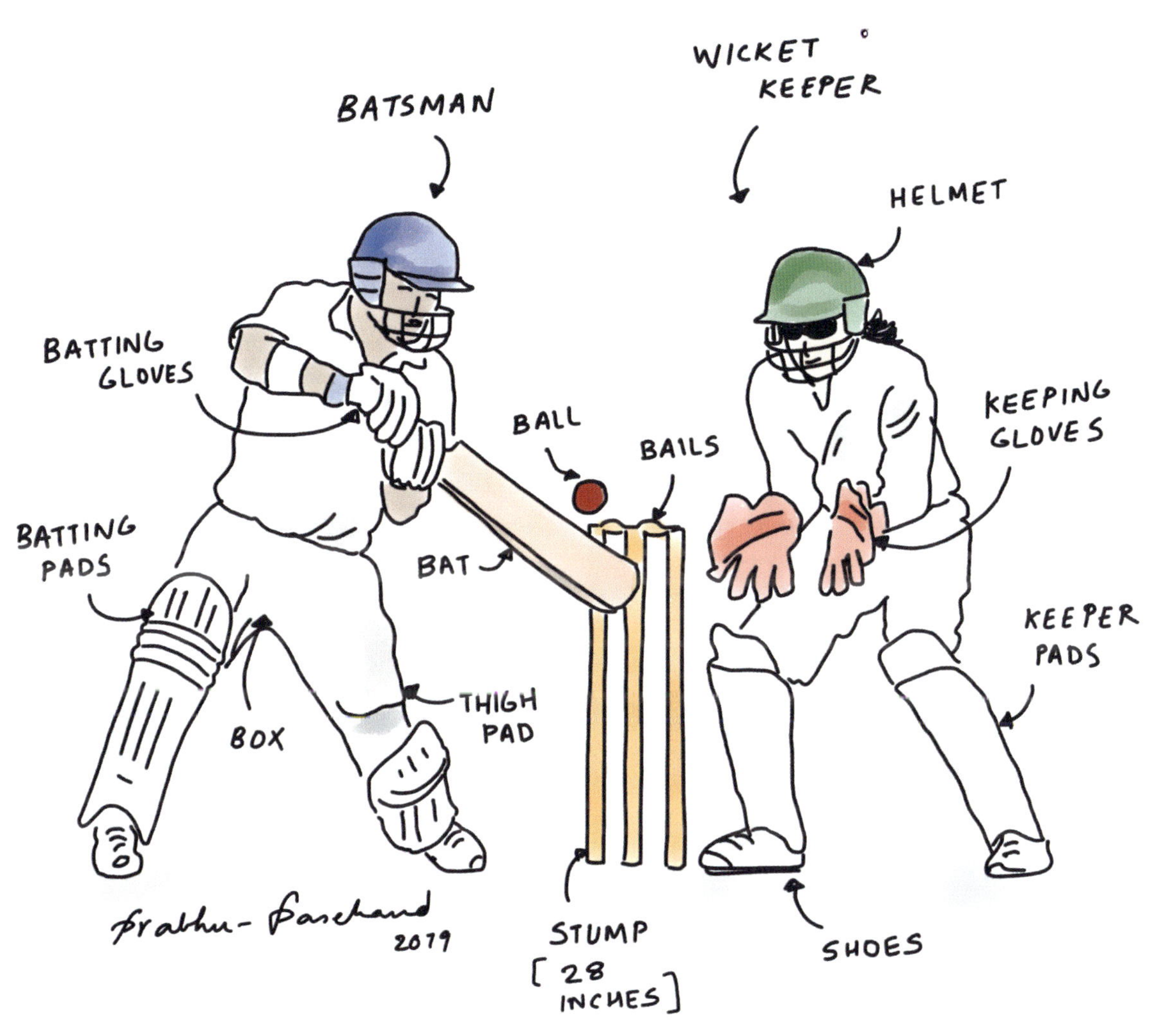
WICKET KEEPER
BATSMAN
HELMET
BATTING GLOVES
KEEPING GLOVES
BALL
BAILS
BATTING PADS
BAT
KEEPER PADS
BOX
THIGH PAD
STUMP [28 INCHES]
SHOES
Prabhu-Ponchand 2019

BATTING OVERVIEW

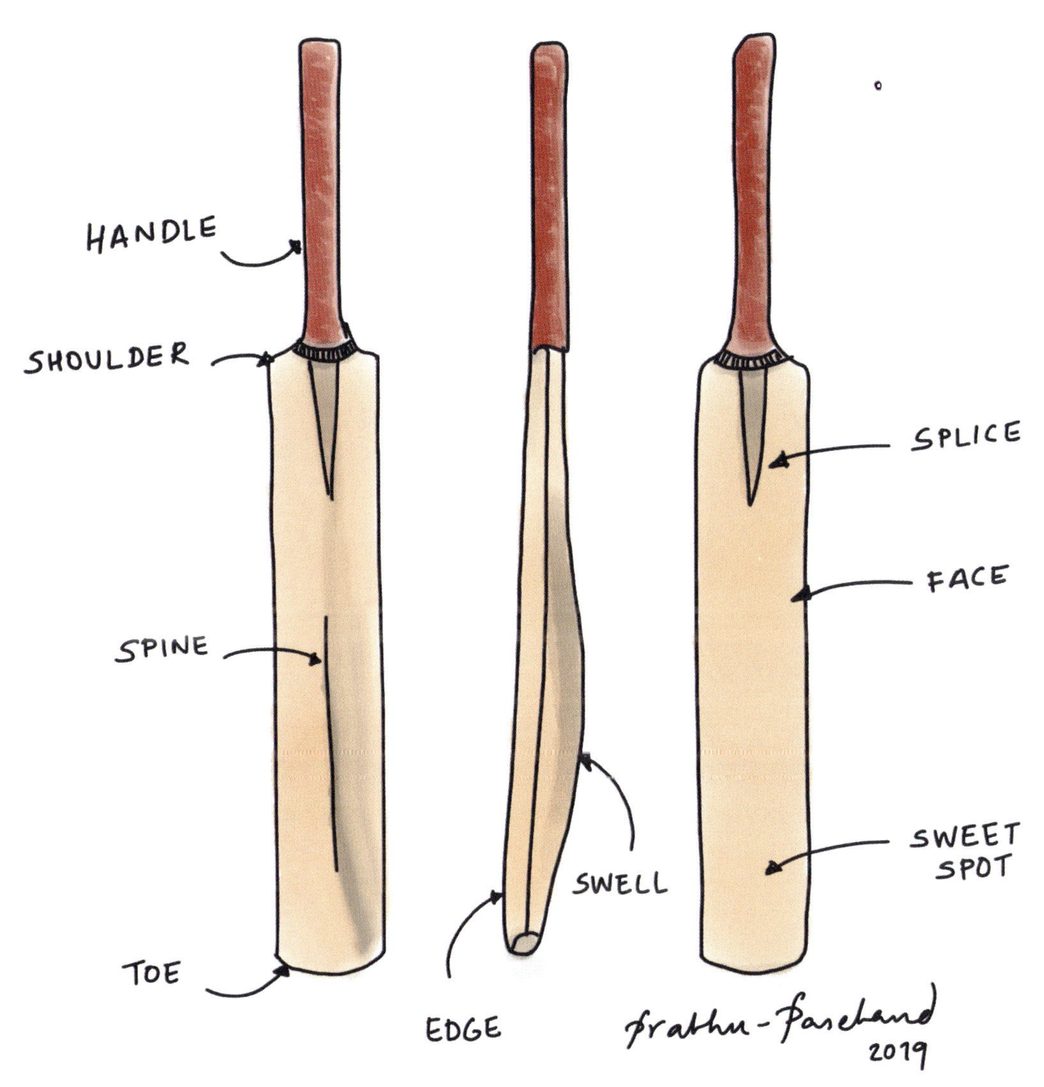
HANDLE
SHOULDER
SPINE
TOE
EDGE
SWELL
SPLICE
FACE
SWEET SPOT
Prabhu-Pasechand
2019

RIGHT-HANDED BATSMAN
LEFT-HANDED BATSMAN
NON STRIKER
BOWLER
NON STRIKER
UMPIRE
UMPIRE

BATTING STANCE
BACKLIFT
SHOT SELECTOR (ATTACK OR DEFENCE)
PLAYING THE SHOT
Prabhu Panchand
2019

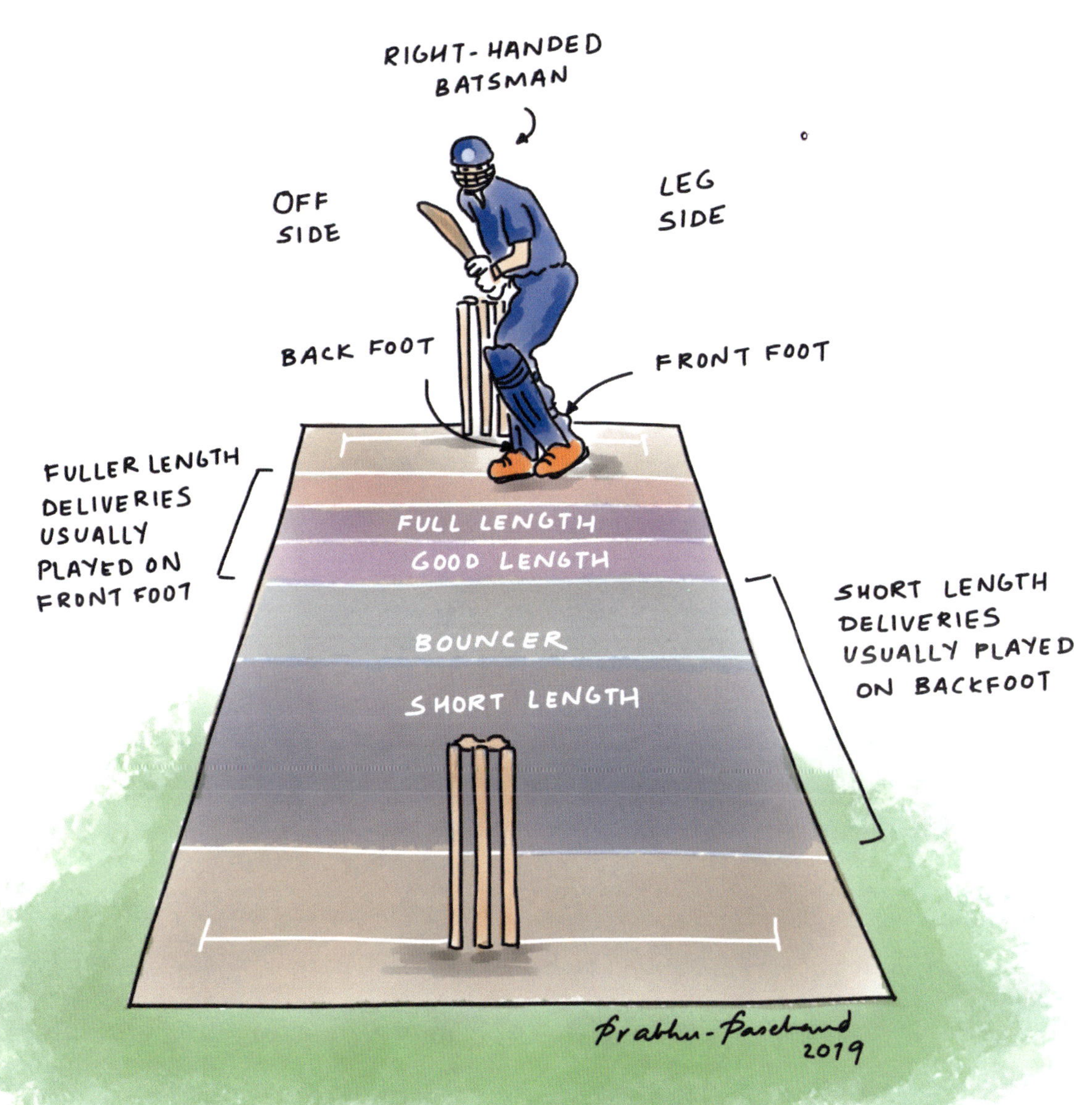
RIGHT-HANDED BATSMAN
OFF SIDE
LEG SIDE
BACK FOOT
FRONT FOOT
FULLER LENGTH DELIVERIES USUALLY PLAYED ON FRONT FOOT
FULL LENGTH
GOOD LENGTH
BOUNCER
SHORT LENGTH
SHORT LENGTH DELIVERIES USUALLY PLAYED ON BACKFOOT
Prabhu-Faschand 2019

RIGHT SIDE : STROKES DEFINED ON FIELD.

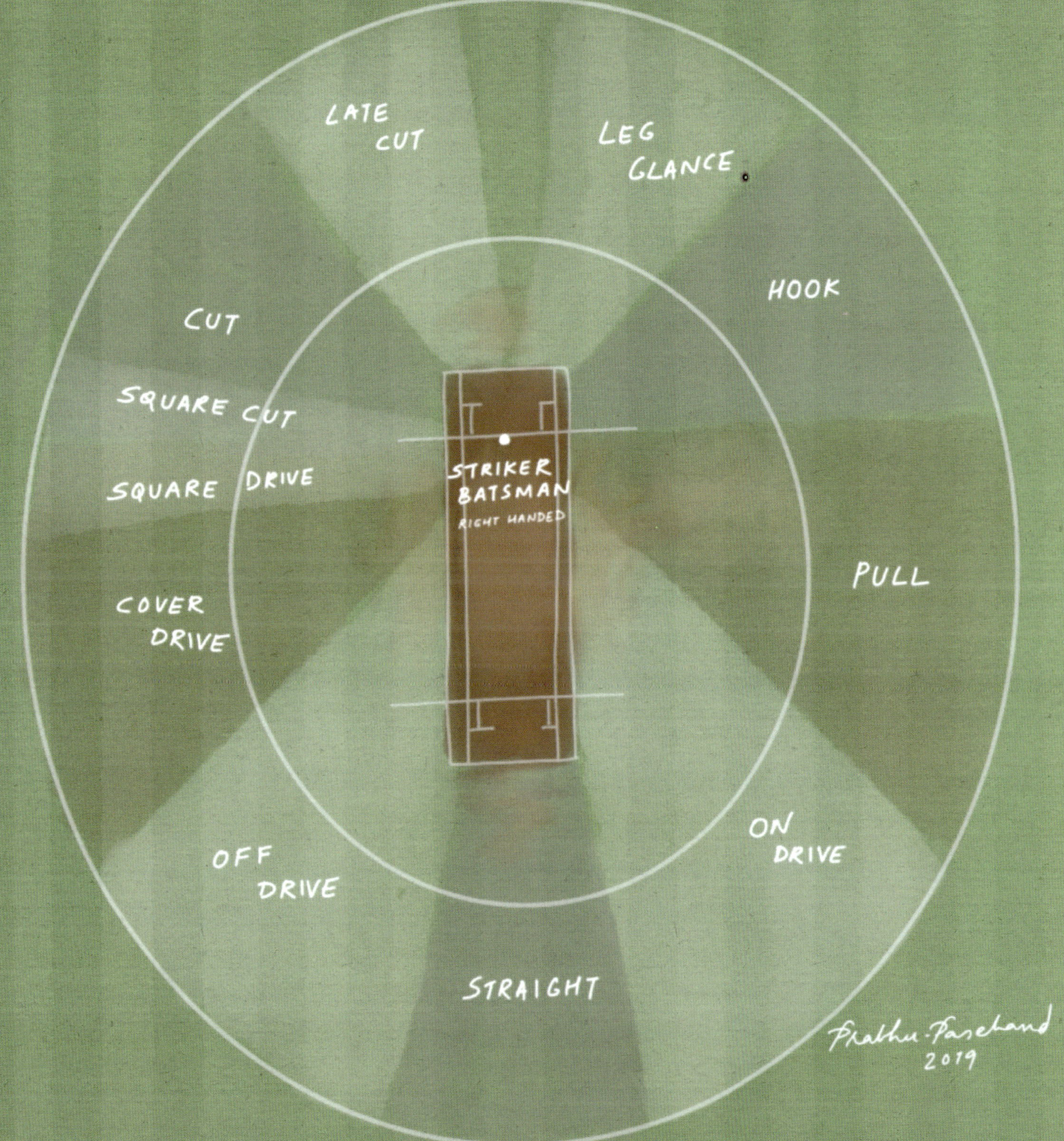
LATE CUT
LEG GLANCE
HOOK
CUT
SQUARE CUT
SQUARE DRIVE
STRIKER BATSMAN
RIGHT HANDED
PULL
COVER DRIVE
ON DRIVE
OFF DRIVE
STRAIGHT
Prabhu-Paschand
2019

UMPIRE SIGNALS

UMPIRES : TWO ON THE FIELD, MAKE DECISION BASED ON LAWS OF CRICKET.

OUT

BOWLED : HITTING WICKET BY A BALL DELIVERED BY A BOWLER.

CAUGHT : IF A FIELDER CATCHES A BALL DIRECTLY OFF THE BAT WITHOUT TOUCHING THE GROUND.

STUMPED : WICKET KEEPER KNOCKS OFF THE BAILS WITH BALL IN HAND AND THE BATSWOMAN IS OUTSIDE POPPING CREASE.

LEG BEFORE WICKET (L.B.W): IF THE BALL HAS PITCHED AND STRUCK PAD IN FRONT OF THE STUMPS.

RUN-OUT : WHEN THE BATSMAN FALLS SHORT OF POPPING CREASE AND A FIELDER KNOCKS OFF THE BAIL THROWING THE BALL.

2019

RUNS SCORED AFTER THE BALL HITS THE BATSMAN'S BODY NOT THE BAT

RUNS SCORED AFTER THE BALL DOESN'T TOUCH THE BATSMAN

BALL DELIVERED WHICH IS TOO WIDE OR TOO HIGH FOR THE BATSMAN TO HIT

BALL WHICH IS DEEMED UNFIT TO PLAY TEMPORARILY.

NO BALL

IF THE BOWLER STEPS OUTSIDE THE POPPING CREASE DURING DELIVERY

IF THE BOWLER HITS WICKET DURING BOWLING

IF THE BOWLER DELIVERS FULL TOSS ABOVE THE BATSMAN'S WAIST

IF THE BOWLER DELIVERS MORE THAN ONE BOUNCER IN THE SAME OVER

IF THE BOWLER CHANGES THE SIDE OF DELIVERY WITHOUT NOTIFYING THE UMPIRE

IF THE BOWLER BENDS HIS ARM DURING THE DELIVERY

D.R.S

DECISION REVIEW SYSTEM

TECHNOLOGY THAT ASSISTS THE UMPIRES IN DECISION MAKING

HAWK -EYE

HAWK-EYE CAMERA

SIX CAMERAS STRATEGICALLY PLACED BEYOND THE BOUNDARY

USES TECHNOLOGY USED FOR MISSILE TRACKING AND NEURO SURGERY.

HELPS THE UMPIRES GET A CLEARER PICTURE FOR L·B·W DECISIONS.

TRACKS THE PATH OF THE BALL AFTER DELIVERY. → MAKES A 3D MODEL OF THE PATH ON AN IMAGINARY PITCH. → PROJECTS THE PATH TRAVELLED BY THE BALL.

SNICKOMETER

MIC ON STUMPS CATCHES AUDIO OF CERTAIN FREQUENCY.

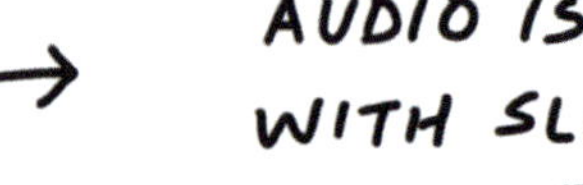

AUDIO IS SYNCHRONISED WITH SLOW MOTION VIDEO FOR CLARITY.

HOT SPOT

USES TECHNOLOGY USED BY MILITARY TO TRACK JET FIGHTERS AND TANKS.

USES TWO THERMAL IMAGING CAMERAS KEPT ON OPPOSITE SIDES OF THE GROUND.

SENSES FEEBLE HEAT GENERATED DURING COLLISSION OF BALL WITH BAT, GLOVE OR PAD. → HELPS BRINGING IN MORE CLARITY WITH RESPECT TO L·B·W

GLOSSARY OF CRICKET TERMS

ALL-OUT - WHEN AN INNINGS ENDS WITH 10 BATSMEN DISMISSED.

ALL ROUNDER - PLAYER ADEPT AT BOTH BOWLING AND BATTING.

APPEAL - SHOUTING AT THE UMPIRE TO ASK IF BATSMAN IS DISMISSED.

BATTING AVERAGE - $\frac{\text{TOTAL RUNS SCORED}}{\text{NUMBER OF TIMES DISMISSED}}$

BOWLING AVERAGE - $\frac{\text{TOTAL RUNS CONCEDED}}{\text{NUMBER OF WICKETS TAKEN}}$

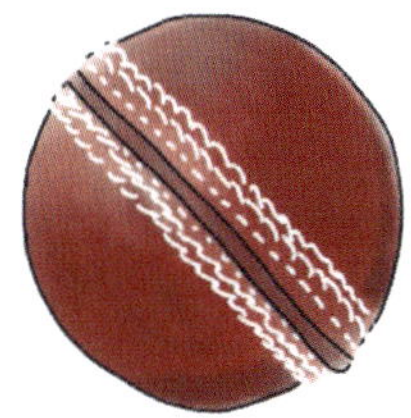

BOWLED - DISMISSAL WHEN BALL HITS THE STUMPS AND BAIL COMES OFF.

CAPTAIN - LEADER OF THE TEAM.

CENTURY - INDIVIDUAL SCORE OF 100 RUNS AND MORE.

COUNTY CRICKET - HIGHEST LEVEL OF DOMESTIC CRICKET IN ENGLAND & WALES.

DADDY HUNDRED - INDIVIDUAL SCORE USUALLY MORE THAN 150 RUNS.

DEAD RUBBER - A MATCH IN A SERIES WHERE ONE TEAM HAS ALREADY WON THE SERIES.

DANCING - BATSMAN MOVING AHEAD IN THE CREASE TO HIT BALL.

DEATH OVERS - LAST OVERS IN LIMITED OVERS MATCH.

DIAMOND DUCK - GETTING OUT WITHOUT FACING ANY DELIVERY.

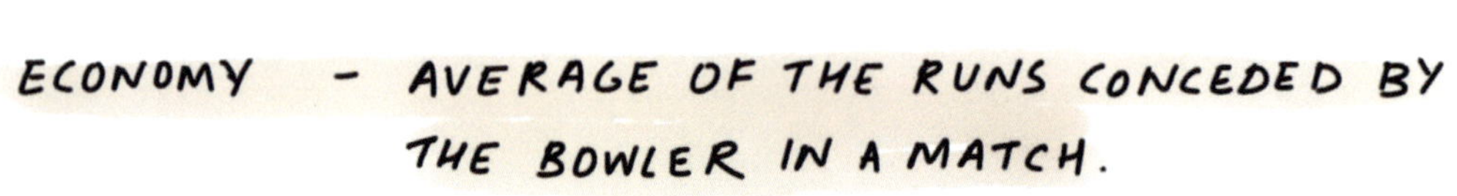

ECONOMY - AVERAGE OF THE RUNS CONCEDED BY THE BOWLER IN A MATCH.

FALL OF WICKET - RUNS SCORED BY THE TEAM WHEN WICKET FELL.

GOLDEN DUCK - BATSMAN GETTING OUT AT THE FIRST BALL FACED.

HALF-CENTURY - INDIVIDUAL SCORE OF 50 RUNS.

HAT-TRICK - BOWLER DISMISSING 3 CONSECUTIVE BATSMEN.

HIT-WICKET - FORM OF DISMISSAL OF BATSMAN WHEN SHE/HE HITS THE WICKET.

L.B.W - LEG BEFORE WICKET.

LEGGIE - ANOTHER TERM FOR LEG SPINNER.

MAIDEN OVER - AN OVER IN WHICH NO RUNS ARE SCORED BY THE BATSMAN.

MARYLEBONE CRICKET CLUB - CLUB THAT OWNS LORD'S CRICKET GROUND. CUSTODIAN OF 'LAWS OF CRICKET'.

MONGOOSE BAT - BAT SPECIALLY MADE FOR T20 CRICKET.

OVER - 6 CONSECUTIVE BALLS DELIVERED BY THE SAME BOWLER.

PARTNERSHIP - NUMBER OF RUNS SCORED BY TWO BATSMEN BEFORE ONE GETS OUT.

RUN RATE - $\frac{\text{RUNS SCORED}}{\text{NUMBER OF OVERS BOWLED}}$

WICKET - DISMISSAL OF A BATSMAN.
or PITCH.
or STUMPS AND BAILS.

Autograph please, old chap!
Prabhu-Panchand
2019

RUN UP
THE BOUND
COIL
RELEASE
FOLLOW THROUGH
2019

-PRABHU-
PASEBAND-

BATTING
STANCE

BACKLIFT

SHOT
SELECTOR
(ATTACK OR
DEFENCE)

PLAYING
THE SHOT

ANJANA WATCHED AND PLAYED CRICKET A LOT. SHE IS OBSESSED WITH THE IDEA OF MAKING IDEAS SIMPLE ENOUGH FOR EVERYONE TO UNDERSTAND AND IS INSPIRED BY THE IDEA OF EXECUTIVE SUMMARIES.

FOLLOW HER @MUSINGSOFABRUSH
OR AT WWW.ANJANAPRABHU.COM

Printed in Great Britain
by Amazon